Copyright 2023
All Rights Reserved

For Felix, Rowan, and Ingrid

I see a bee

A bee sees me

She lives in a hive at the top of a tree
with her sisters – as high up as can be

She flies all day from flower to flower, minute by minute, hour by hour, never stopping, always busy - busy whizzy, whizzy busy

"What's she doing?" I ask my brother.
"I don't know, go ask Mother."

Mum says, "Bees are essential. They have magic powers. Besides making honey, they pollinate flowers".

What's pollination, you ask? It's a very big word – it's a very hard task. Pollination is useful, pollination is neat, it turns flowers into fruit and grains you can eat.

mnm...pie!

So the next time you're eating a blueberry pie or a pizza or doughnut that catches your eye ...

Think of the selfless and hardworking bee who lives in a hive at the top of a tree.

All through the summer, they store honey away and plan long ahead for a cold winter's day.

When they cluster and waggle their wings to stay warm,

to make heat for their queen to weather the storm.

Bees snuggling up on a flower...

Then Spring comes again, and the blossoms come back.

And the bees fly again for a seasonal snack of nectar, the flowers' cool treat. For the bees' endless labor, some sweetness to eat.

I see a bee. The bee sees me.

She lives with her sisters in a hive, as high up as can be.

Bees aren't the only ones who pollinate. Butterflies, hummingbirds and ants also participate. But this story, please, is just about bees, so these other pollinators will just have to wait.

The End

www.ingramcontent.com/pod-product-compliance
Lightning Source LLC
Chambersburg PA
CBHW040024130526

44590CB00036B/84